The Strange God Who Makes Us

Christopher Kennedy

AMERICAN POETS CONTINUUM SERIES. NO. 208

BOA EDITIONS, LTD. * ROCHESTER, NY * 2024

First Edition
23 24 25 26 7 6 5 4 3 2 1

For information about permission to reuse any material from this book, please contact The Permissions Company at www.permissionscompany.com or e-mail permdude@gmail.com.

Publications by BOA Editions, Ltd.—a not-for-profit corporation under section 501 (c) (3) of the United States Internal Revenue Code—are made possible with funds from a variety of sources, including public funds from the Literature Program of the National Endowment for the Arts; the New York State Council on the Arts, a state agency; and the County of Monroe, NY. Private funding sources include the Max and Marian Farash Charitable Foundation; the Mary S. Mulligan Charitable Trust; the Rochester Area Community Foundation; the Ames-Amzalak Memorial Trust in memory of Henry Ames, Semon Amzalak, and Dan Amzalak; the LGBT Fund of Greater Rochester; and contributions from many individuals nationwide. See Colophon on page 87 for special individual acknowledgments.

Cover Art: "To All Believers, Nothing Is Sacred" by Tessa Kennedy
Cover Design: Sandy Knight
Interior Design and Composition: Isabella Madeira
BOA Logo: Mirko

BOA Editions books are available electronically through BookShare, an online distributor offering Large-Print, Braille, Multimedia Audio Book, and Dyslexic formats, as well as through e-readers that feature text to speech capabilities.

Cataloging-in-Publication Data is available from the Library of Congress.

BOA Editions, Ltd.
250 North Goodman Street, Suite 306
Rochester, NY 14607
www.boaeditions.org
A. Poulin, Jr., Founder (1938-1996)

For my mother, Mary Cornelia "Neale" (Behan) Kennedy,

champion speller and lover of music and dance

Contents

III

I

"A"

As a boy, I loved ancient Greece and chose Sparta over Athens. What did I know of the mind then compared to the lure of being carried home on a shield?

We had one volume of a cheap encyclopedia, the kind you buy in a grocery store for 99 cents, letter "A," that had a picture of Achilles in bright green armor, driving his chariot, Hector's corpse, clad in scarlet and dragged behind.

But as I grew older, I found I had no stomach for war. I read the Upanishads, the Four Noble Truths, practiced TM, sought to transcend. I did not transcend. I learned to endure instead.

The mind is not separate from the body, and the body is designed like a car in Detroit with planned obsolescence in mind. I was no warrior, I decided, and heeded the siren call of Athens' ruins.

Me and Question Mark

When a person dies, they turn into music. My father blazed into the ether and came back as Jimi Hendrix's "Third Stone from the Sun." He's distant sounding and immediate at the same time. The swirling guitars explode like meteor dust. The riff that holds everything together reverberates. The first time I heard it, I leaned into the speakers of my cousin's stereo and felt as if someone were speaking to me. I didn't know music was made from souls then.

My friend Dave left early so he could return as *Never Mind the Bollocks Here Come the Sex Pistols*. He's ever present in John Lydon's rants. The rage of a generation induced by my friend's early demise.

My mother slips in and out. Some days she's a person, some days she's music. She's waiting for a few friends in a small town to start a band, so she can appear as the first track on their debut EP. It will be somewhat melodic. A strong, recurring hook will lead to a catchy chorus above a repeated power chord, reminiscent of the early Stooges.

When I die, I plan to go to Mars. The singer from Question Mark and the Mysterians will be there. We're going to form a catchier song than "96 Tears" and travel through outer space to Earth square into the brain of a 15-year-old juvenile delinquent and save him from a life of senseless crime. He'll learn to play the guitar, and he'll figure out the chords that are really me and Question Mark. And then, before you know it, you'll all be dancing.

Of Want and Need

In the dewdrop: a universe. I was told not to look at the sun, and it is all I have ever wanted to do. The locked door, the forbidden forest, the fragile shell: open, walk, hold. I want only what I cannot have.

But need is another story. Need speaks, and I listen. A clumsy dog of love, it enters the room, and I have no choice but to call it to me, pet the uneven fur. But what is need now that want has waned? It used to be I couldn't discern the difference.

Want sings. Need speaks softly and with intent. I want to remember. I need to forget.

Salt

For My Brothers

When I asked you to pass the salt, I still believed there would be many tomorrows. When you asked me if my legs were broken, I thought at first you were concerned.

Now I know you wanted me to be strong. It is weakness that makes us act this way. It is salt that makes the food taste good. It is salt that stings the wound.

Game of Chance

The long hallway was pitch black like the entrance to a funhouse. Mummified in a fuchsia robe, my grandmother sat in an oversized leather chair, her robe pocked with star-shaped burns from her cigarettes.

On the living room wall: a head skewered by thorns. The future kept peeking around the corner to see if I was ready. The Holy Ghost flew by with its tongue of fire like a silent bird of prey.

My grandmother sent me to buy a pack of Marlboros. I ran the whole way, past the dying elms, wary of dogs and Protestants, until I reached the store.

When I came back, out of breath and full of shame, she took the pack and told me to keep the change.

A match flared and a sulfurous cloud rose above her head. I kept myself busy with a made-up game of chance as she smoked and drifted off. I flipped a coin to see if I should warn her as I watched the long ash grow toward her fingers as she slept.

What the Dead Know

It is only the living that can be dreamed of. It is all we know, the rain on their hair, the way they move their hands when they talk. Their bodies on their beds, their voices, the way they sometimes sing. They are so much like birds.

Moving along the sidewalks on their way somewhere important, once or twice a day, they think of us and don't lose their minds and, occasionally, they forget the names of those they love and someone else's name surprises them as they say it, someone they used to love, and they wonder if they still do.

The rooms where they once lay beside them come back with their dark mirrors and white sheets and then they understand how it is that they are touched by the ghosts of every hand that ever held them.

An Aristotelian Summer

For P.L.

Let loose in the sparse hills behind our houses, in the blood-light of an Aristotelian summer, we hid when our mothers stood in our doorways, their sharp voices singing us home for dinner. Days passed all the same. We searched for wood to build a place to go that wasn't home. I corrected something you said once. You hit me as hard as a father. One day, while you were off forgetting, I picked up a rock and threw it to the spot where I knew you would arrive. You were so surprised.

James Dean's Jacket

The Technicolor red one he wore in *Rebel Without a Cause* with his immaculate white T-shirt and pegged jeans. When he stood on the set overlooking the cliff where Buzz Gunderson's '49 Ford took its mock plunge into a dark sheet rigged to simulate an abyss, did he think: icon, myth, legend, or was he too intent on fixing his shy grin as he asked innocently, where's Buzz? whose own jacket proved to be his undoing.

You remember the scene: a game of chicken, the first one to jump out of his car branded with the name his character Jim feared owning, the name he wanted to scream each time his henpecked father wouldn't stand up to his Hollywood ice-queen mother.

And when the race was over—Buzz was down there! down there!—his sleeve having caught on the door handle just as he was about to jump.

More than any scene in the movie, the jacket blazed larger than life, the jacket Jim wore. Or as Plato, Sal Mineo's character called him: Jamie. And Jamie's jacket stood out red as Natalie Wood's lips among the clichéd black leather Buzz and his gang wore, and it stood for Jaime's anger and sexual confusion, his doubts of what it took to be a man, which is why every teen-age boy who watched the movie left the theater thinking less about how to be like James Dean, but rather how a boy finds the courage to wear such a jacket.

Watkins Glen, 1973

Stranded between love and punk, we drove to Watkins Glen to walk the trails and drop a hit of Orange Sunshine or a cap of white mescaline, or both. I stood behind a waterfall and stared at the froth where water poured into water and felt myself leave my body, become the water, move without moving like a seal made of light, as my exhilaration quickly turned to terror when my ego kicked in and said, no, you're a separate thing.

There's a photograph of the moment just before. I'm staring straight ahead. The water looks like a solid sheet of sunlight and smoke. My face so serene and radiant it doesn't look like mine but more like a Botticelli angel's, which is very strange to think about myself, but youth and whatever chemicals were active in my brain gave me a softness I've never had since.

That same year, in winter, we went back and walked the trails, though the park was closed, the trails coated with ice. I was cold and felt the impermanence of being human as I watched the water, a dark gray snake I hoped wouldn't swallow me, but was glad to have a body: flawed, impermanent, and briefly luminous.

The Oracle of Oklahoma City

A waitress with a cloud of gray hair wrangled into a tight bun, who wore pink butterfly glasses, her uniform pinned shut with a nametag that read, "Ruby-my-love," asked me where I was from and where I was going, and when I answered, New York and California, she wanted to know why anyone would want to do such a thing. When I asked what she meant, she said, travel from coast to coast, and I said, I don't know. It seemed like a good idea.

She shook her head, poured my coffee, and sauntered over to the other side of the restaurant where a couple of cowboys sat, elbows on the counter, sponging up yolks with toast, the heels of their boots anchored on the rungs of the stools while they listened to Ruby-my-love as she pointed to my table, still shaking her head.

I sat and pondered the simple question she'd asked that seemed then to be most profound, as if the gods spoke through her, which I knew was a crazy thought but one that kept occurring wherever I happened to be, which oddly enough seemed always to be somewhere between two desirable places, east and west of where I was headed.

Chinese Umbrella

(San Francisco, 1978, after the assassinations of Mayor Moscone and Supervisor Milk)

It was getting dark. The autumn rain had been falling for hours. Storefront windows were a haze of blue light. Streets gleamed occasionally like dying filaments. Cold air drifted in from the bay. In Chinatown, jars of milky gray squids, fetal in liquid, had eyes that examined me as I began to recognize them as my own, my reflection on the glass creating a new beast. Green finches beat their tiny wings against the wooden bars of their frail bamboo cages. Smoke coiled like snakes from sticks of incense. White ash fell. Birds shrieked.

I noticed a red and black umbrella suspended from the ceiling by a braided length of twine like a flower hung to dry. On it there were gold markings painted to resemble fish swimming through reeds. As the umbrella spun slowly around, I watched as the fish moved like thoughts that can't rise to the surface of the mind that has them.

I couldn't hear the rain or the customers inquiring about the prices. My mind was as calm as the imaginary pond. Then I saw the twine that held the handle was frayed. I stepped quickly away as a sudden effusion of light cut through the violet clouds. When I opened the door to leave, the sound of the bell awakened me to a world of slain kings. The rain-soaked streets smelled of tar and sadness as everyone I looked at looked away.

Ithaca

The drive took us south, past two narrow lakes that shimmered and shale beds formed by glaciers, a long, slow time ago. Vines lush with grapes snaked across the trellised fields. A blue heron broke from the banks like pre-history itself.

We passed a winery as it opened its doors to fading sunlight and eager tourists. The caretaker wrapped his tattooed fingers around the handle of a rake and headed to the stone walk to smooth the gray and white pebbles. The heron drifted and disappeared. We noticed the small towns, native names or Greek or Roman, to honor the vanquished or pretend a better fate for ourselves.

The sign for Homer, green and white, appeared at the side of the road. Odysseus came to mind, his journey. But we had been together all those years. I had no point of comparison, no excuse for my absence. No Calypso to blame. The heron reappeared and seemed to hover above the tops of a few old poplars. What did Homer know of loss and longing to invent a story that lasts forever?

Aurora lay west of there where the sun was setting, despite what the name means. I joked that it was sunset in Sunrise, and you were silent. The sun seemed unsure which way to go, stuck there, right at the edge.

Trying to Explain

There is a place inside my longing that no one enters—where a flowering tree opens into unpolluted air—only when I'm alone—glowing in the emerald dark.

The Strange God Who Makes Us

Something in the mother's shrunken, sea-urchin face as she guided her husband's wheelchair along morning rush hour traffic said their lives were worth living, a steadiness in the gaze, as if a distant sea roared from beyond the dull, uneven pavement, an ocean where they could simply merge with whatever world could maintain them better than this one with its seedy laundromats and discount groceries.

The satisfied look on the boy's ash-colored face as he rode his father's narrow lap was as hopeful as the way he tipped his extended arms first right, then left, in imitation of the plane that moved slowly across the impenetrable sky.

Sun gleamed off the diamond patterns of the silver footrests, and one stray wheel, the left front, kept circling inward, pulling the chair toward the curb— the clacking of the wheel like the snapping of small bones.

The stricken father had hands, limp as two dead gulls, that threatened to catch in the rusty spokes but never did, his face honed down to a neo-classical expression: angular, extreme, polished, and hardened like red marble, mythical, as the Greeks might have looked when they imagined tragedy.

The Pure Acceleration of Love

Everything turns to ritual. The cat falls asleep like death on the hardwood floor. An explosion of sparrows bursts across the cobalt sky. The exhilaration of so many wings beating quickly and simultaneously is like a wordless prayer. Even the sound the knife makes against wood as you chop carrots for soup has a rhythm as natural as the birds' soaring, the blade just catching the cutting board as I picture your hand gripping the handle, lifting the blade a few inches above the carrot, then pressing down firmly through the fibrous orange layers, leaving perfect circles, each one larger than the one before it.

There are lessons in these movements, parables written in nature's hieroglyphics that one feels rather than knows, as if the wind as it suddenly begins to well up inside itself, exciting a river of dry leaves into motion, were explaining something to the trees that I can almost understand. And these lessons help me resist the notion that there is nothing human this world can endure.

Buddha spoke of life as suffering and the end of suffering. I used to think he meant all of life is suffering until death, but now I think he meant there are moments when the body's pains and those of the mind vanish as in the passing of the knife through my fears or the scattering of those birds, their wing beats thrumming in the cat's brain as they arc in flight, each one charting a course by instinct or desire, filled with an urge to arrive somewhere it doesn't know, a branch or a wire where it can perch, waiting for some other urge, a hunger or a need, something pure that accelerates inside anything that lives.

A Final Declaration of Faith

A last breath is still a kind of yearning, a final declaration of faith, a last chord in a song too short and better because of it.

An Excuse to Remember

This photograph is a good place to start. Window framed by pale blue curtains, and a streak of red in the night-black glass. This is evidence of the right moment captured and stilled, processed, and cropped.

It's a stranger's room, hanging on my wall. There's an intimacy, almost as if I'm looking at the sunset from someone else's house. I could be a husband, married to the woman who lives there, or a thief, pausing to see something beautiful, and moved by it, deciding to leave what he planned to steal.

And because I have been a lover and a thief, it's easy to imagine the woman's soft, brown hair, the white vanity with its silver broaches and delicate bracelets.

This is an excuse to remember how quiet you were the night I left, the red light in the window that night like the fading red light in the photograph.

I noticed the Bleeding-Heart bush was in bloom when I closed the car door and pulled away.

The Moon, My Loneliness

Along the endless highway that snakes through Wisconsin, tall red cedars line the river, mirrored in the placid surface of the water. And I have driven twenty-two hours to find that the moon exists here as a symbol of my loneliness.

It waits for me in Minneapolis, also, asleep in a swank hotel room, despondent and full. When I arrive, I'm greeted by an affable young man, enthusiastic beyond reason given his station. He hands me two keys and says to feel free to call if I need anything. I want to tell him I need everything and that I am here to reunite with the moon, my loneliness, but I leave him, radiant in his starched white shirt.

Once in my room, I see that the bed is empty. The moon is outside, pretending to be aloof. The Chinese have landed a rocket ship there, too late to matter, eliminating my loneliness exactly not at all. I pull down the shade. It's a given that sleep will elude me, a fact that the sun will replace the moon.

There is a piece of chocolate wrapped in gold on the pillow and a vase of red flowers on the desk. I lie on the bed and point the remote at the TV. My hand on the phone, I can't think of what I want. I can't think of what I want that he can give me.

Slow Seeming at a Distance

A hundred passengers, thousands of feet above the earth without a net, watch a movie, or thumb through a months old magazine, as if in a doctor's office, waiting for results, looking for a mindless distraction.

I can't take my eyes off the plane, its movement, slow seeming at a distance, at an impossible height, through the clouds, a miracle of physics that doesn't require my belief.

When you leave, it will take a while for me to understand. You'll be up there, in miniature, as far away as the memory I have of the time we watched a fly traversing our car. We tried to remember how it was an insect could maintain its flight, why it didn't smash against the windshield, the formula written in chalk on a blackboard in both our pasts, as the oblivious fly lifted and circled, lit, and lifted again, trusting, with no sense of what that means.

At the Supermarket with Russell Edson

How often I think of you, Russell Edson, as I browse the meat aisle and scavenge the packaged limbs for gorilla fists to gnaw on for dinner.

Half-crazed by fluorescence, I remember when you asked the hotel clerk for 200 keys. Her face was the face of all of America, confused, rattled, a little stupid with expectations far from the world as it is. I still fell in love with her. Something about her smile said more than biannual trips to the dentist for cleanings. Once I'm done shopping, I plan to drive straight to the hotel to propose to her, or whoever works the 3 to 11 shift these days.

I imagine you, Russell, one of twelve children, a cartoon life in Darien, pushing a cart though the IGA, while Muzak castrated a popular tune of the era as you followed the scuff marks of those who shopped before you, devising your escape through a logic only you could imagine.

But what's this? No gorilla fists? The world's not the same without you, Russell. A man can't cook his favorite stew these days. I'm surrounded by chicken, and pork, and beef. Not even a pig's knuckle to hold me over until the primates are back in fashion.

When I check out, I'll do it myself, and leave inconspicuously, my head full of dreams and thoughts of the wife I don't have, berating me for forgetting something I didn't know I needed.

II

Memory Unit: Pregnancy Scare

On the way to the hospital, my 92-year-old mother tells me she can't be pregnant. I've never even dated, she says. I don't know what to say. I explain that she's deficient. Vitamin B. Precautionary measures. But when I check her in, the woman at the desk says she'll need to go to the 5th floor, the psych ward, where she spent a few weeks a few months before. The doctor asks her to disrobe, and she tells him she's not pregnant. He seems impatient, unwilling to humor her. I tell her it's all right. No one thinks you're pregnant. The doctor composes himself. He's red-faced, on the verge of anger. A nurse appears with a hospital gown, tells my mother to put it on. Why? my mother asks, near tears. I take the gown from the nurse and set it down on the metal table next to where my mother sits. She'll be fine, I say. The nurse seems about to speak, then thinks better of it. She looks at the doctor. They leave the two of us alone. Now what? my mother asks. I don't know, I say. She says, the least you could do is ask me to dance.

Memory Unit: Braids

I push the button for the elevator and wait with a woman in a wheelchair and her nurse. The woman holds a cloth Raggedy Ann doll. She strokes the orange yarn, braided to resemble hair, with fingers that are mostly bone. The doors open. I see my face reflected in the polished elevator wall, a skull with dark circles beneath its sockets.

Yesterday, I was good at smiling. My mother spent our visit talking to me as if I were her brother Tom, home from flying reconnaissance over Anzio. When I looked out the window, I saw a man with an oxygen tank, sitting on a stone bench, smoking a cigarette.

Today my thoughts braid and unravel, the dull repetition of what my mother utters from her mouth makes twilight in my brain. I stare at the picture of me and my siblings, hung on the wall to remind. I'm the youngest. I have a nervous smile, as if I can see the future.

Memory Unit: Broken Record

My mother insists she's half here and half not here. I feel like an empty dress, she says. I feel like a wig but no head. She thinks I'm her brother, home from World War II. I wonder if she's met my father yet, or if she's still at home, fighting with her sisters over their one good dress. Or is she further back, on Tompkins, looting the shelves of her grandfather's grocery store, in the days of prosperity before the crash. Where do I live? she asks. What am I supposed to do?

Nothing. I tell her she's supposed to do nothing. It's all taken care of, I say, and she looks around the room for her purse as she stuffs tissue after tissue into the pockets of her robe. I feel like an old shoe, she says. I feel like a broken record. She pats her white hair and says she needs to have it done. I can't go out looking like this, she says. She says, I feel like I can't remember. She tells me all her children are dead and asks me again who I am. I tell her I'm her youngest. She smiles and says you wouldn't kid me, would you? I say, no. I wouldn't. I don't.

Memory Unit: Your Face Looks Familiar

If you didn't come here, I wouldn't know a thing. I never heard of this before. At least I'm talking about it now. Tell me your name again. You're here to help me, right? I used to be Catholic, but not anymore. I'm dead. This is hell. There's nothing on TV anymore. The woman next to me never says a word. What am I supposed to do? Tell me your name again. Your face looks familiar. Do you think we can die? I know I can't go to heaven. Did you bring these pictures? I don't know what I'd do if you hadn't come here. It's awful to be alone. I don't have a memory. I'm 92. How old are you? You're young. I wish I knew what to do. Who's this again? My son? I remember red hair. I remember my wedding day. And my husband. My brother Bill. What did he do? Is he dead? It doesn't bother me. Tell me again who you are. You look so familiar. I remember the face, but I've never seen you before.

Memory Unit: Family Portrait

The nurse tells me it's a good idea for my mother to look at pictures. The nurse is perky, means well. Has the type of blonde hair that signifies cheerleader or dental hygienist. I understand she's doing the job she's trained to do. She thinks it's a good idea to help my mother remember the past. I don't know how to tell her my mother's past is exactly the kind of thing you want to forget. I don't know how to tell her it's better this way, the bad memories, fading to black.

I think of the day I looked over my uncle's shoulder at the picture of my father's car, crumpled, on the front page of the morning paper. My mother, a fixed smile on her face, walking from mourner to mourner, comforting them, not yet able, it seemed, to feel the blade-pierce of grief that would twist inside her the rest of her life.

I thank the nurse, take the picture of my siblings and me and hide it on top of the wardrobe. We're smiling, though the photographer was hours late, and we were angry. My oldest brothers have removed their ties and sport jackets. We're smiling because the photographer said something ridiculous to make us laugh, and we laugh, even though we don't think it's funny.

Memory Unit: Ornithophobia

A bird lands outside the window. No reaction. Okay, I think, okay. Her fear of birds, gone, another gift. I remember how she would pause at the doorway, head covered with scarf or newspaper, while the birds, ignoring her, went mad, as if trying to map the nightfall sky with their wings, a manic attempt to find meaning, each bird held to its path as the mad whorl banked and dipped, wound itself into the sky. My mother, shielding her eyes, missing it all, stuck in her invisible cage, calling to me, her voice pitched with terror, a song like the voice of a child, who, seeing a bee, is afraid of being stung, having been stung many times before.

Memory Unit: Praying in Hell

I'm dead. That's why I'm here. And I'm never going to die. That's how my mother explains her circumstances today. And my husband is in heaven. I'm in hell. She points at her rosary, pale blue, a child's gift at First Communion I imagine came from the gift store downstairs. I should throw that away, she says. Why? I ask. I shouldn't have it in hell. It's okay, I say unconvincingly. Who's going to take care of me? I am, I say. Aren't you going to die? she asks. I'm silent. She thinks she's dead and can never die. What should I say to calm her? I'll never die? I'll die but not soon? We look at each other, each of us lost in thought. She says someone should write a book about this. I laugh. She laughs. I haven't lost my sense of humor, she says. No, you haven't, I say. Keep these, I say and offer her the beads. It's okay to pray? she asks. I don't know what to say.

Memory Unit: I Have a House

My house is green with black shutters. There is a red Japanese maple. Blue hydrangeas and purple irises. White daisies. The waxy leaves of the bayberry. Sumac trees line the edge of my back lawn. My mother sits in her wheelchair at the nursing home. I tell her these things about my house, which she has never seen and can't imagine. She frowns and indicates she can't hear me. Holds her hand up to her ear. The more I raise my voice to tell her the details of my life the more she strains, the more the details seem unreal, a story I'm making up to help her understand the world she no longer grasps.

I realize I'm doing this not for her benefit but for mine. I'm here, I keep saying. I exist. I have a house. Trees and bushes. Flowers. Some poison berries.

Memory Unit: Self-Employed Actor

Have you noticed I don't get any older? My mother's vanity intact, she's pleased that time stands still in hell. There's nothing for me to do except agree, reprise my role as benevolent demon. It's a perfect scenario, the two of us in the hell we've both made, my mother the wide-eyed child, me the reassuring parent. How else could it end except as a repeated performance, my mother speaking her lines like a pro and me ad-libbing, thinking on my feet. A self-employed actor in hell.

Memory Unit: The End of the World

Today I visit my mother in the lounge where she's hunkered in her wheelchair as she eats lunch with some of the other residents. They are arranged in a circle around a gray plastic table where they resemble a flock of some type of bird, their faces more avian than human. Some of them clutch stuffed animals like dead prey. Some drool and moan. There is a man at the table today. A rarity. He's about my age. The least sentient of the flock. I stand next to my mother and ask her how she feels. She smiles, then winces. I ask again. She cups her hand over her ear. I ask a third time. She winces. The man begins to tremble. The other members of the flock are staring at me. They smile. One of them points at me. My mother winces. The man begins a guttural moan that sounds like the end of the world.

I walk to the elevator. Push the button. Wait. The woman in the wheelchair with the Raggedy Ann doll waits next to me. The sound the man makes grows louder, until there are no other sounds. I push the button again. Wait. Wait. Wait. The woman wheels her chair toward me. She says something I don't understand. I don't look at her. If she were telling me the meaning of life, and all I needed to do was bend my ear toward her to hear it, I would not be able to do it. There is only one sound. It is the end of the world.

Memory Unit: Black Chicken

I remember the black chicken. My mother and I had a war of wills. There was a pan on the stove for weeks in the kitchen on Yorkshire. I was twenty, and she kept asking me to empty the pan, and I kept refusing for some reason I can't remember. My friend John asked what was in it and lifted the lid, releasing the satratoxins before I could stop him. The stench from the mold caused John to drop the lid so he could cover his face with both his hands. What were we fighting about? Why was I so stubborn? Why was she? I finally relented and carried the pan out back, emptied it in the tall grass on the hill near the purple iris. We laughed about it after, but now it's my memory alone. I see it in my mind's eye, carbon black and lethal. Funny that it comes to me now, after all these years. Too late to say I'm sorry for what she can't remember.

Memory Unit: The Game

When my mother asks me how old she is, I tell her as old as the yellow paint on the walls in this timid light. And she laughs and asks me who I am again, and I ask her if she can tell me the names of her children, and she can, in order of their births, and she laughs again, and I ask her if she knows which one I am, and she says no and laughs, and I laugh, too, because it's funny, this game we play when I visit and try to find out what she remembers and what's been erased, and I can almost see behind the dampness in her eyes to the images of me that disappear one by one, like a string of Christmas lights, flickering on and off, burning out.

Memory Unit: Blank Slate

Almost a blank slate, my mother lifts her head from sleep. Her mouth hangs open, her nose stays pressed against her cheek. As if she's made of clay, waiting to be reformed. She looks at me as if for the first time. I'm one more stranger who visits, who claims to be someone he cannot possibly be. The television, sound down, flickers in front of her. She looks at me, then at the TV. Nothing much on, she says. I nod. We watch together what neither of us understands.

Memory Unit: Buddha Mother

My mother refuses to die. Out of fear, I imagine, or, I imagine, out of stubbornness. Or maybe she's forgotten about death. She's forgotten everything else, why not the thing that keeps the rest of us awake at night? Maybe she just can't remember that the body's a temporary place. Could it be she doesn't know she has a soul? Her rosary beads lie under her pillow like a coiled snake, but maybe she's forgotten how to pray. Or maybe she prays differently now. It could be she's transcended the need for words arranged as a plea to an invisible god. Maybe she's closer to the source now and there's no need to think of herself as a thing apart from other things. My mother the lotus blossom. My mother beneath the Bodhi tree.

Memory Unit: October Cemetery

My mother and I did this every year. We drove to Snyder's Florist on the other side of town and bought a potted plant. Begonias maybe, or marigolds, some type of flower, whatever was cheapest, whatever we could afford. We continued to St. Agnes's and drove through the black, iron gate with the ornate lettering. It made me think of angels. Maybe there were angels on the gate. Maybe I associated the gate with heaven. Every year on the anniversary we did this and every year it was the same result. We circumambulated the cemetery's narrow cinder-strewn road and never, not once, did we arrive at my father's grave. I kept quiet the entire time, my mother moving from silence to a kind of angry, grief-stricken wail and attendant tears.

One time, the last time, as we completed our second lap around the grave markers, I spoke. I said, we need to find it this time. My mother looked confused, as if I'd violated a pact, the one that required my assent to be part of this Sisyphean task. Why? she asked. I told her, so I'll know where to bury you.

Memory Unit: Wedding Day

My mother points to her wedding photo and says that's me, that's your father, and that's my brother, Bill. There's Rita, her friend from long ago. The rest she doesn't know. Every visit another person disappears, as if the chemicals that stilled the moments of her past have begun to burn them. It's trick photography, an image here one minute and gone the next. They're black and white. I try to imagine the colors they wore and realize they were exactly that: black and white. A wedding day. The bride and groom. Exactly as they were. Waiting to disappear.

Memory Unit: John and Gladys

Do you remember John and Gladys? My mother thinks the names sound familiar. They should. How do I say this? Zeus and Hera of my youth. Grandparent surrogates. My mother's saviors. I say, remember when John brought a lake trout he caught into our living room? Remember Gladys on her hands and knees, scrubbing our floors to relax? Or the story of Gladys in a tug of war with a rat at Lilac Manor, her husband's one good shirt between them? Or the cake of ice in the toilet in winter? The hole in the ceiling that showed the sky?

She doesn't remember. I go on. Story after story, and I realize how much I miss them, John and Gladys, the stories, the nights at home when they visited, my mother laughing as if nothing bad has happened, as if the night could last forever, the silver-bellied fish on the rug, the scrub brush and bright yellow bucket on the kitchen floor.

Memory Unit: After the Funeral

The phone rings early Saturday morning. It can only be one thing. The day after the funeral, I go to the nursing home to retrieve the few belongings my mother has left behind. I bring a large garbage bag to gather her clothes, grab the photographs and the drawing of three ballerinas my daughter gave her. I wait for the elevator. The woman in the wheelchair is singing a lullaby to her doll. The doors open. Hush, little baby. Hush, little baby.

Memory Unit: Diorama

I broke the lock on the green metal box I had taken from her closet before she moved into the nursing home. I lifted the lid and inside there was another box, a diorama of some kind, and in it, in miniature, a replica of my childhood home, situated on my old front yard, complete with two weeping willows, a white birch, a catalpa, and my mother, dressed in an outfit I remembered from an old photograph: yellow slacks; powder blue sleeveless blouse; royal blue kerchief. And next to her, my father, in white T-shirt and work khakis, his silver hair combed back off his sunburned forehead. Inside the house, four silhouettes: my brothers and sister, shadows of a kind.

In the catalpa, I saw myself, a boy with close-cropped hair, shirtless, in a pair of ragged shorts. Above me, both in the photo and in the box, a blue sky full of clouds, white as my father's shirt. No sign of the impending storm.

Memory Unit: Outer Space

A few months after my mother's death, my three-year-old granddaughter tells me her dream. She's in outer space. She sees a sad computer. Mr. Spaceman Astronaut Computer, she asks, why are you sad? The computer says, because you are related to a shooting star. I say, that's a great dream, as I think of how we are all related to shooting stars, a remix of carbon molecules, as strange and important as the sun.

III

The Perfect Syntax of Rain

My house is a nest for every flying thing, and summer won't go away as it should, as it spreads its own dry and yellow wings across the sky.

It could be the night has forgotten all of us, our memories erased, and no one knows what the stars are trying to say, all tricked out with light, or that the sky should be slick with rain as the wind carries away the leaves.

But the wind carries nothing, the air is still and eerily warm, as if it, too, has forgotten to be itself the way a painting can't remember paint.

It's still good to be alive, and when the perfect syntax of rain finally arrives and reminds me of the womb, then my dreams will manifest a bright green lizard in the sink.

Tonight, the sweetness of apples is a constant memory, dirt in the folds of my skin when I bend my wrists. The moon is saying something to the sun. Maybe a request for more light.

The moon is huge, and it doesn't matter. Its light is borrowed and has no power. I desire a river or a storm, a different way to remember the past.

I was strangely happy then, when I used to listen to the creek rush by at night and feel what it's like to know exactly what to do. Grateful for my moonshot of a life, I sang with many tongues from my throat of unspeakable dark.

Climate Change

Sure, we breathe in the history of the world, the air that everyone else has breathed before us, the rain once an ocean, our blood and bodies mostly water. But if we are the result of fish that learned to crawl and grew honeycombs inside their chests, then my hands were once fins and therefore frighten me.

Is that why Christ broke bread with fishermen? If I nail a fish to two pieces of wood, does that constitute a sacrifice?

I don't mean to offend. I'm stuck on what it means to be human. Are we heaven-aspiring mimics of some celestial design gone wrong? Mutants whose cities should have risen underwater, our borders changing with the tides?

It's warm today like the inside of a shoe. Though I should be turning the heat on this time of year, I'll lie in bed with the windows open instead tonight, and in my dreams the sea will come calling and wash its shells and pink anemones over my human body, and I'll wake suddenly, as if about to drown.

Random Destiny Notebook

The era of the mini apocalypse is here. In a superstore parking lot, a dozen cars are circling for the last place to park. The authorities are herding a few shoplifters to their cruiser. Freedom, you're a melting ice cream cone in a small child's fist, and I'm rooted here like a weeping willow.

When I close my eyes, a familiar darkness appears. It's the least I can do to ameliorate the status quo. Later, I'll write that down in my random destiny notebook for future generations to discover.

But I'm tired of having to do everything. O black rose of spent time, soon we'll stop hiding our corpses and admit they're part of a cottage industry. We'll build new prisons out of bone and round up our secret enemies. We'll play the music of the spheres on instruments made of flayed skin. We'll admit the love of money is not a sin but a birthright and elect a president made of gold. The one who finds the parking space will rejoice. Celebrity judges agree!

Creation Myth

Late spring, and the parched earth can't quench its thirst. The astounding clouds and disorienting shadows turn alien everything I know. Whorls secure the tight buds on the wild anemones beginning to bloom. The retention pond has receded, the cattails wave back and forth in the stiff breeze. The white barn looms. The swayback has no shadow. The cliff swallow guards her nest and swoops down from the birch tree. Watching from the window, I'm startled by my own eyes. Two blue eggs about to hatch.

Parable

I sent back the angels you sent me and bought a pile of bones. From it, I built my own angels. Heavy and without wings, they stay put and shadow no one. I always know where to find them. I gave them common names and expected nothing from them. If one dared lift a sword of fire, I would steal it and send them to heaven, disarmed and ashamed. Let God concern Himself with such a traitor.

My angels are made of bones. They laugh out loud when someone mentions the soul. They are not the least bit religious. When they get sad, they drink and fight amongst themselves. They have no time for human dramas.

Every so often, their sadness is too much to bear. That's when I visit and remind them of the reason for their existence. You are here to make me feel less lonely, I tell them, and they perk up. Some of them attempt to fly. No, I tell them, that's not your job. But we are angels, they say, and I'm forced to watch as they attempt to please me but fail to reach the sky.

The Devil's Workshop

It doesn't take long to get here. A few days of nothing to do, and inertia turns the mind so far inward I can imagine the place where evil sets up shop, where perfect angels fit their joists with such precision that I should be amazed and eager to learn their craft, but it's indolence that brought me here, not ambition.

I'll just watch, thank you, as they build their flawless death ships, the machinery of chaos and confusion, rigged with seamless sails, the convoluted warp and weft of fear.

That evil never rests is not surprising, that it makes so much so beautifully, hardly a terrible shock, but why then pick an idle mind to set up shop? Why not the fertile brainwaves of those whose minds aspire to a higher plane? Or is that the trick?

The boy who spends his days in front of the blue-light of the computer screen, eating junk food, suddenly turns off the monitor and grabs the rifle from beneath his parents' bed.

Let those who seek redemption grow weary, while those who'd rather nap are factories for plots of random terror. A neat frustration for any who like a side order of meaning with the meat of their lives.

In the devil's workshop, they whistle while they work, content in their knowledge that though they've fallen, as sure as God has a plan, the devil has his blueprints, and chaos, when it's fashioned right, is as perfect as the light of any heaven.

The Nest

It appeared overnight, a turban-shaped sculpture of disquiet. Impassive now, at dusk, in the corner of the eave, it waits to unleash its bald-faced inhabitants. Stuck there, an imperious thing no one should disrupt. To fear it makes sense. If one pokes it with a stick, it vibrates, an electric hum shoots through it: winged, copper aliens form a line of pain. The fear-inducing buzz, the venom of each sting, all to defend a queen in repose. They circle, then drop, as they find the target: a pale, monstrous creature of unimaginable size.

Spring Cleaning

I raise the blinds to greet the dead flies, struck again this year by the luminous green surfaces of their metallic bodies. (Or as Roy Orbison used to sing, "Only the lonely know the way I feel tonight.")

As I carry away each desiccated husk, I think of my friends and my parents, who never had wings, reduced now to memory, fading as the last light fades each night.

The neighbor's Christ-flowers bloom early this year, their purple blossoms stark against the ice-covered hills of snow that surround them.

After gathering the flies together, I remember that sometimes flies are dormant not dead, a concept I've never understood, and there's no way to know which state they're in.

Buoyed by the thought of a possible resurrection, I pile the flies on the desk and wait.

Forensic Prediction

Whale-shaped clouds loom above the retention pond. I hear the mechanical whirr of the spreaders as they spin like a carnival ride across the drought-baked lawns. I open the door, see a nest, defenestrated from eave to stoop. A cloud of poison in the injured air.

Finished, the workers load the spreaders onto flatbeds, then stab the ground with plastic warnings. A deer zig zags past the pond, disoriented, and almost hits my car. How red the blood will be where the deer lies dying in a flattened circle of yellow grass.

In the Distance

There's a mystery in the distance, a few stick figures, scarecrows maybe, telephone poles, depending on how far away they are. Now the mystery builds, the speculation. What if it's obvious, and I'm the only one who doesn't recognize? Today is shaping up to be like every other day, I guess. Maybe trees? Leafless, a few bare branches. Maybe something I've seen before but no longer remember?

I have a few friends to ask, but how do I know they won't tell me what I want to hear (my fear of scarecrows, my love of trees) and lead me in the wrong direction (out of love, mysterious thing). I may wait until the sun goes down. See if anything lights up (a region in my brain?). There's always tomorrow, too, the living say somewhat foolishly, but I need to decide soon. It looks like rain. Everything looks like rain.

Strange Planet with Hostile Atmosphere

What an utter pleasure to be in this line that never moves but affords me an opportunity to see, really see, the world for what it is, a mixture of deafening vehicle sounds and a chemically infused sunset, preternaturally red and black, like the hide of a dormant mythical beast as it rises from sleep.

I've been here so long I've forgotten whether I was on my way somewhere or on my way back from somewhere else. I like this feeling. It's as if I had been dropped from a spaceship and forced to learn the customs on a strange planet with hostile atmosphere.

I have my hands on the wheel, the blue dials glowing in front of my eyes, anonymous car horns urging me forward despite the impossible nature of that request. Soon, I'm going to go, begin my expedition, discover the flames and rubble of a self-destructing civilization. Plant a flag known to mean: I give up.

The Last Romantic

When gas was under $2 a gallon, on my way home from the last visit to my mother in her nursing home, I drove to the hillside near my house to watch traffic stream by on the bypass where a doe slept in the bullseye of grass, encircled by the highway.

Above me, a hawk searched for mice, lifted its wings and, catching an air pocket, hovered like death's angel.

I didn't see the kill, or the doe, shattered by a fender, but I knew the hawk succeeded, and I found the doe by the roadside, a thread of dark red blood across her muzzle.

What else was there to learn? I drove away, resisting the nervous urge to check for messages, and entered the bypass carefully, yielding to the faster vehicles.

Saved

A chimpanzee was saved from a man who bought him from traders. The man trained the chimpanzee to perform a parlor trick, which the man charged people to see.

The chimpanzee learned to strike a match and light a cigarette with it. He smoked the cigarette, much to the audience's delight.

The men who saved the chimpanzee from the man brought him to an island refuge and weaned him from the cigarettes.

The chimpanzee's life is much better now. He's safe from mistreatment and eats bananas. But every day he walks on the beach and gathers a few small sticks. He puts one in his mouth, and the others he scrapes against a rock, hoping to create a spark.

So that Night Can Fall

These are my horses. They fell from the sky. We can ride them if it ever gets dark enough. Close your eyes infinitely, so that night can fall, too. Then we can wear the stars as crowns.

Edict

Oblivion we solo.
  —Roger Fanning

Maybe it's as simple as our brains seize up on what our retinas can't filter, all the colors of a new century too bright and garish, a neon flood that sears, its soundtrack a remix of familiar tunes above an incessant beat. Or maybe, now, life is a death sentence we're willing to serve. I can only guess. But hopefully the sea brings comfort, and I'm glad you can live there.

Maybe it's a matter of being where you know the roads and currents, where you can watch the rain swell in strong winds, and water implies the ease with which we all could drown. Think of it this way: the past was someone else's future, electric and disturbing, and still they persevered. Let's not wait another million years to say hello. Remember, too, that we both know how to swim.

Doubt

If it's true we crawled up from the bottom of the ocean, then our skulls are seashells, our hands starfish. As we lie here in bed, it's as if we have washed up on a white beach.

If it's true, then what prayer is there for me to say and to what presence do I owe this moment? These bodies, then, the ocean surging within them, might be all we will ever have. So, when we invent a god, we give it flesh and hope something more lives inside.

Such grace we wish for ourselves, too, as we fall asleep, listening to each other's breath, softer and softer, until a different ocean whispers in our ears.

Poem for Shang Qin

Though we've never met, I've been digging my way toward you since the day I was born. The lamplight outside my window turns to diamonds and I think of you. A dog barks in my sleep, and I dream of you eating figs under a banyan tree. I look at the sun. I think, what is the old master doing right now? Cursing the darkness? I'm alone, looking at a painting and thinking, what would you think of all this purple?

I love tomorrow because I know you're already there, walking along with your strange shadow, changing your name to save your life.

A Painter's Light

These days, I exist only to exist, the way children exist in their rooms among their toys, as the light through their windows, silted with dust, creeps over them, a painter's light they never notice.

Ancient. That word rises through the mind's endless strata. The light of paintings in antiquity is purer than the light today. The light in the short film about the painter I watched last night both obscures and illuminates as she points to the pink flowers in the trees.

In later frames, the clear light accentuates the flowers she now wears in her dark hair. I want to know the name of those flowers: Black Locust? Red Poppy? But the film is silent. The film is silent. The room is quiet. The light fades.

The flowers wilt. The painter dies but lives on when the light projects her on the screen. These days, I exist only to exist.

This is my life story, then, the French film of my desires shot in black and white and subtitled, projected on the wall. A pile of books from floor to ceiling, the harsh rectangle of light from my computer screen. Empty cans. Faint music. A song I used to hum I never learned the words to.

Occlusion in Long Rain

For my father

What the world spoke today was not the world but what I thought of it. Six days of rain. Through my blurred slice of window, I saw a fragment of what there is to see. How small I am. How large to notice that space among spaces.

And shortening my vision, I saw my face in the window and remembered my dream of you in a phone booth on the side of a desolate road, rain obscuring your face, dripping down the glass.

Even now it's hard to close my eyes. Hard to know the body is mostly water, that we disappear except in dreams.

And so, the world today is a row of trees, a line of parked cars, and a gray unyielding sky. And a life is nothing more than rain, and nothing less.

The Coda

I used to ride my bike past the local night club on summer afternoons and watch the jazz musicians smoking in the parking lot out back. It's been torn down for years now, the musicians surely dead. So, too, the beautiful woman with the towering beehive, who lived across the street, who loved country music and always seemed to be adjusting her bra, a gesture I think of now as a public act of love, blinking in memory like the neon sign above the club.

I once opened the wrong door in a funeral parlor and saw a dead man, his face pulled back, the ropelike muscles beneath the flesh there for anyone to see.

Every day, I rode as far as I could with my eyes closed, the wind more present that way as it slapped my face and told me I could never die.

A boy believes everything he's told and spends the rest of his life unlearning most of it, but some nights I can hear the blue notes of the saxophone cutting through the dusk and see the moon listing like a sad canoe over The Coda, nights when I close my eyes and there is no wind to lie to me.

Acknowledgments

Cimarron Review: "The Pure Acceleration of Love";
Cream City Review: "Chinese Umbrella";
Dreaming Awake: New Contemporary Prose Poetry from the United States, Australia, and the United Kingdom: "A," "At the Supermarket with Russell Edson," "Random Destiny Notebook," "Slow Seeming at a Distance";
North Dakota Quarterly: "The Devil's Workshop";
Ploughshares: "Occlusion in Long Rain";
Plume: "Poem for Shang Qin";
Porlock: "Parable";
Prism International: "The Strange God Who Makes Us";
Red Brick Review: "The Oracle of Oklahoma City";
Stone Canoe: "The Coda," "What the Dead Know";
Tampa Review: "James Dean's Jacket";
The Progressive: "Climate Change."

Thanks to Peter Conners and the crew at BOA Editions, Ltd.—Justine Alfano, Kathryn Bratt-Pfotenhauer, Sandy Knight, and Isabella Madeira—for all their assistance in the making of this book.

Thanks to my daughter, Tessa, for her wonderful artwork.

Thanks to Stephanie Scheirer and Sarah Harwell for their friendship and willingness to read this book before it was a book.

Thanks to Peter Johnson and Danny Lawless for their support.

About the Author

Christopher Kennedy is the author of *Clues from the Animal Kingdom* (BOA Editions, Ltd., 2018), *Ennui Prophet* (BOA, 2011), *Encouragement for a Man Falling to His Death* (BOA, 2007), which received the Isabella Gardner Poetry Award, *Trouble with the Machine* (Low Fidelity Press, 2003), and *Nietzsche's Horse* (Mitki/Mitki Press, 2001). He is one of the translators of *Light and Heavy Things: Selected Poems of Zeeshan Sahil*, (BOA, 2013), published as part of the Lannan Translation Series. His work has appeared in many print and on-line journals and magazines, including *Ploughshares*, *The Progressive*, *Plume*, *New York Tyrant*, *Ninth Letter*, *Wigleaf*, *The Threepenny Review*, *Mississippi Review*, and *McSweeney's*. In 2011, he was awarded a National Endowment for the Arts Fellowship for Poetry. He is a professor of English in the MFA Program in Creative Writing at Syracuse University.

BOA Editions, Ltd. American Poets Continuum Series

Colophon

BOA Editions, Ltd., a not-for-profit publisher of poetry
and other literary works, fosters readership and appreciation
of contemporary literature. By identifying, cultivating, and publishing both new
and established poets and selecting authors of unique literary talent, BOA brings
high-quality literature to the public.

Support for this effort comes from the sale of its publications, grant funding, and
private donations.

*The publication of this book is made possible, in part,
by the special support of the following individuals:*

Anonymous

Blue Flower Arts, LLC

Angela Bonazinga & Catherine Lewis

Bernadette Catalana

Daniel R. Cawley

Margaret B. Heminway

Nora A. Jones

Paul LaFerriere & Dorrie Parini, *in honor of Bill Waddell*

Barbara Lovenheim

Joe McElveney

John H. Schultz

Sue Stewart

William Waddell & Linda Rubel